Good Answers to Tough Questions

WITHDRAWN

Trauma

Joy Berry

Illustrated by Bartholomew

Joy Berry Books
New York

Joy Berry Enterprises
146 West 29th St., Suite 11RW
New York, NY 10001

Cover Design & Art Direction: John Bellaud
Cover Illustration & Art Production: Geoff Glisson

Production Location: HX Printing, Guangzhou, China
Date of Production: February 2010
Cohort: Batch 1

Printed in China
ISBN 978-1-60577-507-4

This book can provide good answers to tough questions about:
- Trauma and traumatic experience
- Trauma that is your fault
- Trauma that is not your fault
- Negative reactions to trauma
- Positive reactions to trauma
- Handling trauma that is your fault
- Handling trauma that is not your fault
- Facts about trauma

Life is pleasant much of the time, but sometimes it is not. Sometimes your body gets hurt.

Sometimes your feelings get hurt.

Some kinds of pain you experience do not hurt very much. Other kinds hurt a lot.

Physical or emotional pain that hurts a lot is called trauma.

Anything that causes trauma is called a traumatic experience.
Here are some examples of traumatic experiences:

- Serious illness
- Serious injuries
- Staying in the hospital
- Death of someone you know or love
- Divorce in your family
- Remarriage in your family
- Moving
- Going to a new school
- Being separated from your family
- Losing something that is very important to you
- Repeating a grade in school

TRAUMA THAT IS YOUR FAULT

Who is responsible for the trauma you experience?

Sometimes you are responsible for causing the trauma you experience.

You can cause trauma by disobeying the rules.

As long as you live, there will be rules for you to follow. Some rules have been made to protect you and your belongings.

When you disobey these rules, you might hurt yourself. The pain that you experience can be traumatic.

Some rules have been made to protect other people and their belongings.

When you disobey these rules, you might have to experience painful consequences. The pain that you experience can be traumatic.

Some rules have been made to protect the things around you.

When you disobey these rules, something might happen that hurts you. The pain that you experience can be traumatic.

TRAUMA THAT IS NOT YOUR FAULT

Sometimes you are not responsible for causing the trauma you experience.

Sometimes people do something that hurts you. The pain that you experience can be traumatic.

Sometimes you get hurt when something happens that you have no control over. The pain that you experience can be traumatic.

Trauma that happens to you when you break the rules is your fault. You are responsible for causing it.

Trauma that is caused by other people or by situations that are out of your control is not your fault. You are not responsible for causing it.

You can prevent a certain amount of trauma from happening to you by following the rules. However, you cannot completely prevent trauma.

No matter who or what causes the trauma you experience, it will have an effect on your life. Whether trauma has a negative or positive effect depends on how you react to it.

Your reaction to trauma is negative if you
- believe that you are helpless.
- develop a fear that keeps you from growing and becoming a better person.
- begin to worry in a way that keeps you from living a happy, healthy life.
- develop angry feelings that make you unhappy or cause you to become sick.
- become exhausted and depressed.

Your reaction to trauma is negative if you believe that you are helpless.

No one has complete control over trauma. No one knows exactly when it is going to occur. No one has the power to completely avoid trauma. When something traumatic happens, you may feel out of control. Feeling out of control can cause you to believe that you are weak and helpless. Believing that you are weak and helpless can keep you from doing the things you need to do to grow and become a better person.

Your reaction to trauma is negative if you develop a fear that keeps you from becoming a better person.

Trauma can be extremely unpleasant. Most people want to avoid it because of the pain it causes. Once you have been hurt by a traumatic experience, you might become afraid that it will happen to you again. This kind of fear can make you overly cautious. It can keep you from doing things you need to do to grow and become a better person.

Your reaction to trauma is negative if you begin worrying in a way that keeps you from living a healthy, happy life.

Most people do not want to experience trauma. When you do not want something to happen, you may begin to worry that it will happen. Worrying takes a lot of time and energy. When you are worried, it is hard to do the things you need to do to live a healthy, happy life.

Your reaction to trauma is negative if you develop angry feelings that make you unhappy or cause you to get sick.

Trauma can disrupt your life and keep you from doing the things that you need or want to do. This might frustrate you and make you angry. Also, trauma might seem unfair. You might feel as though you are experiencing pain you do not deserve.

Anger is a powerful emotion. If it lasts a long time, it can make you very unhappy. It can also cause you to become sick.

Your reaction to trauma is negative if you become exhausted and depressed.

Fear, worry, and anger can waste a lot of your energy. If you experience these feelings for a long time, you can become exhausted. It is very difficult to do anything when you are tired. Doing nothing can cause some uncomfortable feelings. You can become frustrated. You might feel guilty. You might become depressed.

Your reaction to trauma is positive if you
- learn valuable lessons.
- become more caring and kind.
- become more confident.
- begin to appreciate the good things in your life.

Your reaction to trauma is positive if you learn valuable lessons from it.

You can learn something from the trauma you cause. You can learn why the rules exist and why you should obey them. You can also learn something from the trauma other people cause. You can see the mistakes they have made, and you can learn to avoid making the same mistakes.

ONE THING I LEARNED FROM THE ACCIDENT IS THAT IT'S IMPORTANT TO WEAR SAFETY BELTS.

I'VE LEARNED THE LAB IS NO PLACE FOR A MONKEY.

Your reaction to trauma is positive if you become a caring, kind person.

When you experience trauma, you can learn how other people feel when they experience trauma. This can help you care about other people who are hurting. It can help you be kind to them. When you care about others and are kind to them, they respond in a positive way. This can make you feel very good.

Your reaction to trauma is positive if you become a more confident person.

When you experience trauma and survive it, you can begin to believe that you are strong and can handle almost anything that happens to you. This confidence can help you overcome the fear that can keep you from living a normal, productive life. It can also make you willing to do the things you need to do to grow and become a better person.

Your reaction to trauma is positive if you begin to appreciate the good things in your life.

If you were to have nothing but good experiences, you would probably take them for granted. You would most likely expect only good things to happen and would not value them. When you do not value something, you might not benefit from it as much as you could if you valued it properly.

Sometimes a painful experience helps you learn to appreciate the good things in your life.

If the trauma you experience is to have a positive effect on your life, you must learn to repond to it in a positive way.

Here are six steps for handling trauma that is your fault.

STEP ONE: FACE IT

Admit that you are experiencing trauma. Admit that you are in pain. Don't pretend that you are OK.

STEP TWO: ACCEPT IT

Accept this fact: the trauma is not going to go away immediately. Realize that you are going to experience some pain for a while.

STEP THREE: THINK ABOUT IT

Find out the answers to these questions:
- What did I do to cause this trauma?
- What consequences will I have to experience?

STEP FOUR: DECIDE WHAT TO DO

Find out the answers to these questions:
- What do I need to do to make the people I may have hurt feel better?
- What do I need to do to make myself feel better?

Make sure that the things you decide to do are not harmful to you or others.

STEP FIVE: DO WHAT YOU HAVE DECIDED TO DO

If you have hurt other peple, you need to do all you can to make them feel better. Make sure that you

- admit that you have done something wrong.
- say that you are sorry.
- do everything you can to make up for your wrongdoing (make sure that your efforts are acceptable to the people you have hurt).
- try not to do the same thing again.

You also need to make yourself feel better. Make sure that you

- remember that you are a human being (you are not perfect, and it is normal for you to make mistakes).
- forgive yourself when you do something that is wrong.
- learn whatever you can from the situation.
- try not to do the same thing again.

STEP SIX: TALK ABOUT YOUR THOUGHTS AND FEELINGS

Your trauma can cause you to have many thoughts and feelings. It is important that you do not ignore them. Pay attention to them. Share them with someone else. When you talk to someone, you need to make sure that the person is

- someone you respect and trust.
- someone who cares about you.
- someone who is old enough and wise enough to help you.

This person might be:
- A parent
- A guardian
- A teacher
- A counselor
- A principal
- A clergyman
- A close relative (such as grandparent, aunt, or uncle)
- An adult friend

Keep talking about your thoughts and feelings for as long as you need to. Talking about a traumatic experience one time will probably not make everything OK. It might take six months or even a year for you to feel better about trauma you have experienced.

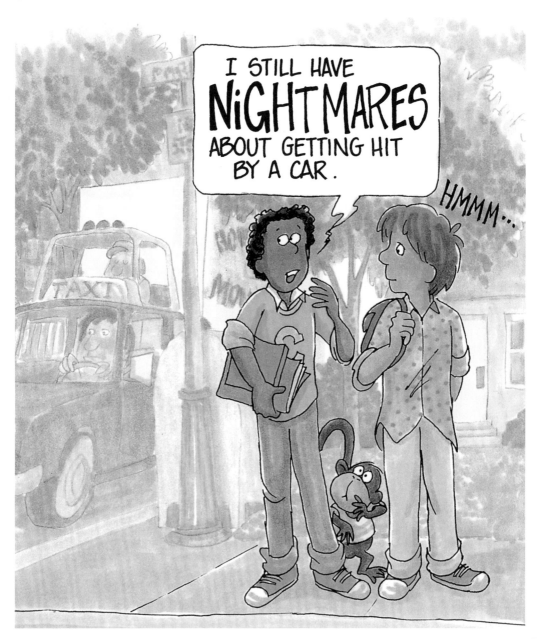

Here are six steps for handling trauma that is not your fault.

STEP ONE: FACE IT

Admit that you are experiencing trauma. Admit that you are in pain. Don't pretend that you are OK.

STEP TWO: ACCEPT IT

Accept this fact: the trauma is not going to go away immediately. Realize that you are going to experience some pain for a while.

STEP THREE: THINK ABOUT IT

Find out the answers to these questions:
- What happened to cause this trauma?
- What is going to happen to me?

STEP FOUR: DECIDE WHAT TO DO

Find out the answers to these questions:
- What can I do to make the situation better?
- What can I do to make myself feel better?
- What can I do to make the other people who are involved in this situation feel better?

Make sure that whatever you decide to do is not harmful to yourself or to others.

STEP FIVE: DO WHAT YOU HAVE DECIDED TO DO

If possible, you should
- talk to the people who caused the trauma (if you cannot talk to them, talk to someone else).
- try to understand why these people did what they did.
- try to forgive them.
- do not blame yourself in any way.
- do whatever you can to make yourself and the other people involved in the situation feel better.

STEP SIX: TALK ABOUT YOUR THOUGHTS AND FEELINGS

It is important that you continue talking about your thoughts and feelings until you feel better.

It will be easier to handle trauma if you remember these four facts:

Fact #1. There are some good things about every situation. Try not to focus on the bad things about a situation. Instead, look for the good things and focus your attention on them. This will make you a happier person.

Fact #2. Things could always be worse. Try to realize that no matter how bad a situation seems to be, it could always be worse. Be thankful that it is not worse. Being thankful will help you feel better.

Fact #3. Every problem has a solution. When trauma creates a problem for you, try not to waste your time and energy feeling bad about it. Instead, realize that your problem has a solution. Spend your time and energy finding the solution. This will help you overcome the problem and feel better.

Fact #4. "This too shall pass" and "time heals all wounds." "This too shall pass" means that, as time passes, every experience comes to an end. "Time heals all wounds" means that, as time passes, your trauma will most likely become less painful, and you will feel better and better. When you experience trauma, remind yourself of these two sayings. Doing so will help you remember that at some time the experience will be over, and you will feel better again.

Trauma can have a positive or negative effect on your life. It all depends on how you react to and handle it.